# THE CAT
# ZODIAC

THE CAT ZODIAC

An Hachette UK Company
www.hachette.co.uk

Summersdale Publishers Ltd
Part of Octopus Publishing Group Limited
Carmelite House
50 Victoria Embankment
LONDON
EC4Y 0DZ
UK

www.summersdale.com

Printed and bound in the Czech Republic

ISBN: 978-1-78783-233-6

Substantial discounts on bulk quantities of Summersdale books are available to corporations, professional associations and other organizations. For details contact general enquiries: telephone: +44 (0) 1243 771107 or email: enquiries@summersdale.com.

# THE CAT ZODIAC

*A Feline Guide to Astrology*

**MAGGY GREYMALKIN**

summersdale

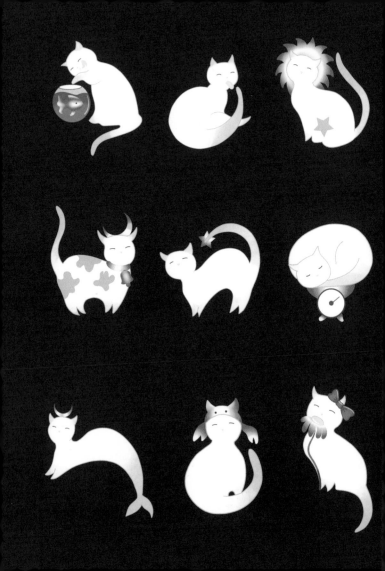

# Contents

*A dog jumps into your lap because he's fond of you; a cat does the same because your lap is warmer.*

**A. N. WHITEHEAD**

# INTRODUCTION

Long have humans looked to the stars for guidance in their lives. Sometimes, Jupiter itself needs to enter their chart in a kind of cosmic dance for them to decide whether they'd like to be a coffee barista instead of a florist, or whether those trousers they bought are showing too much ankle. With all this planetary planning going on, it's natural these humans may forget to ask: "But what about the destiny of my cat?"

After all, are cats not born in the same calendar beneath those same twelve signs? We may not wish to make coffee, or care about ankles. We may, on the surface, seem to care about very little at all. But we have higher paths, greater purposes, truer callings, and this book serves as a guide to ensure you are set to make this *your* year.

Of course, your human will probably want to help you achieve this, and they may do so in the same way they help you each and every day: by mostly staying out of your way and just letting you get on with it.

I'D BEEN TOLD THAT THE TRAINING
PROCEDURE WITH CATS WAS
DIFFICULT. IT'S NOT. MINE HAD
ME TRAINED IN TWO DAYS.

# THE SIGNS OF THE ZODIAC

### Aries
Bold; ambitious; enthusiastic

### Taurus
Stable; practical; patient

### Gemini
Adaptable; affectionate; curious

### Cancer
Intuitive; loyal; resilient

### Leo
Lavish; warm-hearted; passionate

### Virgo
Intelligent; analytical; hard-working

### Libra
Cooperative; gracious; diplomatic

### Scorpio
Magnetic; protective; resourceful

### Sagittarius
Optimistic; generous; idealistic

### Capricorn
Disciplined; determined; sensitive

### Aquarius
Independent; inventive; clever

### Pisces
Compassionate; intuitive; wise

*Cats are smarter than dogs.*
*You can't get eight cats to*
*pull a sled through snow.*

JEFF VALDEZ

# THE ELEMENTS

## *Fire signs*

### Aries

### Leo

### Sagittarius

Fire signs are enthusiastic, courageous
and bold. They're always ready to instigate
something new. Usually trouble.

........................................................

## *Earth signs*

### Taurus

### Virgo

### Capricorn

Earth signs are strong, determined and practical.
They're focused on seeing things through
and aren't afraid to get their paws dirty.

## Water signs

**Cancer**

**Scorpio**

**Pisces**

Water signs are friends, lovers and nurturers. Their only issue with people-snuggles is not getting enough of them.

........................................................

## Air signs

**Gemini**

**Libra**

**Aquarius**

Air signs are thoughtful, sociable and honest. As long as you haven't disturbed a nap.

**CATS CHOOSE US,**

**WE DON'T OWN THEM.**

*Kristen Cast*

# ARIES

## 21 MARCH – 19 APRIL

**Symbol:** The Ram
**Element:** Fire
**Ruling planet:** Mars

**Gem stone:** Diamond
**Colour:** Red
**Lucky number:** 1

# **PERSONALITY**

## *Overview*

You're the first sign of the Zodiac, and being a leader is not something you shy away from. You're charismatic, brave, strong: a leader of cats and humans alike. Your eagerness to see yourself as flawless and invulnerable can rub some up the wrong way, but don't worry: you're persuasive, assertive and charming. You can always explain why they're wrong.

★ **Best traits:** Courageous; determined; honest.

★ **Worst traits:** Too courageous; too determined; too honest.

★ **Likes:** Being challenged; taking charge; "turning life up to 100".

★ **Dislikes:** Slowing down; taking orders; being ignored when they've made it clear that that hand should go nowhere near them.

★ **Strengths:** Boldness; magnetic personality; ability to lead.

★ **Weaknesses:** Following others; being moody/childish.

# **RELATIONSHIPS**

## *Friends and enemies*

Let's face it – you are not a conservative cat. "Faint heart never won fair feline" is a changeable sort of phrase you apply to pretty much whatever you're doing. Those under the sign of Taurus are not wired like you. They like to look before they leap; you simply leap and deal with the landing when your paws hit the ground.

What you need is someone who can keep up. You like things done quickly, impulsively and adventurously. Find yourself a Gemini to match your explorer's spirit and zest for knowledge. When you must fearlessly squeeze yourself down some unknowable hole in the garden on nothing more than a whim, trust your Gemini ally to be right behind you.

## Love and sex

That Virgo you've noticed around the neighbourhood might be swaying their tail, rolling their shoulders and purring as they pass, but know this: their nature is to analyse their partners intensely, some of which includes criticizing and finding fault. And you're way too good at love and sex and relationships to have to listen to that.

This may seem blindingly obvious, but, if you can each keep your pride in check, a self-assured, lascivious Leo will be your love-match. With your fur sleek and shiny, your chests puffed out and your heads held high, you're practically mirror images: a kind of two-cat interpretive dance. It's meant to be.

## With humans

Being a cat, you don't have an awful lot of money, but if you *did* you can bet you'd be flicking notes, one by one, from the stack in your paws with reckless, sexy abandon. That makes you less than compatible with the cash-conscious Capricorn model of human. They have "pennies" to save, and are unlikely to understand your perfectly valid reasons for snubbing the expensive scratch-post they bought you an entire boring week ago. The best person for you is a Sagittarius. They have bags of energy, a devil-may-care attitude and they love to have fun and frolic – they're just as likely to chase that mysterious red floor-dot as you are.

# RISING STARS AND PLANETS

You are ruled by the powerful Mars, and you start the year with its full power behind you. So walk tall, swish your tail, lick your paws and brush your fur just how you like it, and watch everyone take note of you. But be aware: as Mars enters Libra in the first weeks of October, your drive and confidence might wane. This is the time to fake it 'til you make it, and no sign does it quite like you.

# HOROSCOPE

"Go hard or go home" is a phrase that could be the Aries motto, and that drive and energy will stand you in good stead. Nervy friends, though well-meaning, might try to give your grand dreams an early bath. Don't be deterred. Whether your goal is to bring home more dead animals than you managed last year, or to be the next swaggering, slow-motion feline for the biggest cat-food companies, this is your year!

# TAURUS

## 20 APRIL – 20 MAY

**Symbol:** The Bull
**Element:** Earth
**Ruling planet:** Venus

**Gem stone:** Emerald
**Colour:** Green
**Lucky number:** 23

# PERSONALITY

## *Overview*

Resilient, strong, practical, friendly – you're the sign everyone can rely upon. You can be safely passed at close range by other cats and safely petted by humans, as long as they respect your routines and don't bring chaos to your life. Chaos, like serving your dinner an hour later than you'd like it.

★ **Best traits:** Sensual; patient; warm-hearted.

★ **Worst traits:** Rigidity; stubborn resistance to sudden changes.

★ **Likes:** Relaxation; dependability; luxury (not so good for the human who buys your food).

★ **Dislikes:** Change; unpredictability.

★ **Strengths:** Trustworthy; considered; loyal.

★ **Weaknesses:** Obstinate; inflexible; possessive.

# RELATIONSHIPS

## *Friends and enemies*

Aries are thought of as being fun, but not when your idea of fun is "prudent" and "considered". You like luxury, you *love* catnip, but you measure it out to last; an Aries huffs it in one go and spends the next hour being off-the-wall crazy.

If you want someone who really gets you, look no further than Capricorn. These cats enjoy security and enjoy having it by relying on savings. So when that Aries is scowling and moody because their catnip is in the red, you and your star-crossed bestie will have plenty left to make your days a joy.

## Love and sex

An Aquarian's aloof, detached demeanour will clash with your loyal, sensitive side. They're also unpredictable and love to experiment sexually, while you know what you like and are content to stop there. Every night will be a new way to make your basket rock, when all you want is to have the lights out by ten.

Look to Cancer for a bit of what you need: empathy, sympathy and a love for building deep, long-term relationships. While others mewl and scrap in the dead of night, your energies can jointly focus on what's important in life, like the unending number of things you can watch through the window.

## With humans

You're considered. You're relaxed. You like to live a good life at a measured pace: traits which bring you into direct conflict with Gemini humans. Their love of spontaneity and variety and their high-energy style will leave them constantly trying to get a rise from you, and leave you plenty of time to practise your flat, unamused stare.

Pisces people enjoy peace, beauty and music, and this is where you cross into harmony. Other signs watch your little cat-face spinning around-and-around beside a turning record on a deck and think you're baffled. Your Pisces person knows you're just both super into The Jam.

# RISING STARS AND PLANETS

Your ruling planet, Venus, goes through zero retrograde phases this year. Great news for the two areas of your life that she commands: wealth (or fish/catnip) and love. This could mean your human finally getting that promotion and showering you with treats and nibbles galore. And with January bringing you soothing energy from a Venus/Jupiter crossover, you've got pawsitive vibes coming your way.

# HOROSCOPE

Perhaps last year had you a little distracted, spread a little thinly trying to please too many others, and you didn't give as much time and energy to your loved ones as you may have wanted. Now is the time to focus on your inner circle. This is the year for giving a quick meow-dee-doo to those you barely know, and for rubbing your cheek glands all over your bestest ones and reminding them how much they mean to you.

# GEMINI

## 21 MAY – 20 JUNE

**Symbol:** The Twins
**Element:** Air
**Ruling planet:** Mercury

**Gem stone:** Blue sapphire
**Colour:** Yellow
**Lucky number:** 19

# **PERSONALITY**

*Overview*

The sign of The Twins is a real charmer. You're super sociable and you've got the gift of the gab: while some cats might cry over spilled milk you're always on hand to offer perspective. Some cats, especially potential mates, may think your playfulness can at times border on childishness. But it's okay, because they just smell like old fish.

- ★ **Best traits:** Communicative; intelligent; enthusiastic.

- ★ **Worst traits:** Brash; fickle; and (*gulp*) curious.

- ★ **Likes:** Friendly cats; friendly humans; change; freedom.

- ★ **Dislikes:** Hissy, unfriendly cats; boredom; staying in one place.

- ★ **Strengths:** Cunning; versatility; independence.

- ★ **Weaknesses:** Short attention span; indecision; restlessness.

# RELATIONSHIPS

*Friends and enemies*

Being under the sign of The Twins, communication is your strength. You consider issues from both sides and speak your conclusions freely. Beware, then, the sensitive Pisces. If, in your considered opinion, their new collar is a fashion disaster, you're bound to tell them, and they're bound to slink off somewhere dark and hate you for days on end.

Your duality can also cause paralyzing indecision. You're an ideas cat. Should you run up and down indoors, or go outside where there's more space (but for some reason you don't feel the urge to run in it)? This issue, and many others, can be solved by a bold, go-getting Libran. You're the perfect pair – you set them up and your Libra knocks them down.

## Love and sex

You know those cats on MewTube that creep up behind other cats and frighten the life out of them? That's you. And the scaredy-cat is Taurus. Tauruses aren't afraid, not at all, but they're considered and practical and like to plan, and you're spontaneous and unpredictable and like to spring the day's itinerary on them before they know what the day even is. Don't do that to a Taurus. Just don't.

You know who *would* appreciate those qualities? Aries. You're both energetic and independent, and can spend your days separately prowling the streets and eating food at multiple humans' houses. But you also have the assuredness to know who you want to share your bed with at the end of the day.

## With humans

Leo humans are too precious to make good housemates. They lead you into the lounge and reveal they've bought you the most amazing... thing. They place "the thing" in front of you, with a big grin on their face. Ta-daa. And it's not that you don't want it, it's more that you haven't figured out what it is yet. And while you think, with what appears to the uninitiated human as a disinterested stare, their Leo pride gets hurt and the "offending" mystery is removed. Hiss. No good.

A Sagittarius person matches your skills of considering, forgiving and forgetting. They think deeply and are unlikely to be hurt by your reflection on strange gifts you're expected to love immediately. Forgiveness comes easily to you both, and this is your great bond: you can forgive them for leaving you outdoors just a little too long, and they can forgive you for lying on their keyboard when they have a deadline in an hour. Purrfect.

# RISING STARS AND PLANETS

You're a social animal as it is, but when the sun enters your sign in late spring you'll be supercharged! You'll be chatting at the door to be let out, chatting at the window to be let in, chatting outside the bedroom for your breakfast. Your human is going to love it. As a water sign, your intuition will be key this year. Go with your gut, and make that elegant leap!

# HOROSCOPE

Being under the sign of The Twins, coupling comes naturally to you. Generally, you like to strike up a rapport, have your whiskers tickled and sashay off to the next pretty thing. But this year will be your year for stronger connections, for building a partnership that lasts. This year, you'll be more concerned about finding someone who *is* the cat's pyjamas, rather than simply focusing on getting those pyjamas off.

# CANCER

## 21 JUNE – 22 JULY

**Symbol:** The Crab
**Element:** Water (*hiss*)
**Ruling planet:** The Moon

**Gem stone:** Ruby
**Colours:** Silver and white
**Lucky number:** 3

# PERSONALITY

## Overview

Beneath that tough, protective exterior is a loyal and reliable individual, and a calm communicator who puts others at ease. When it comes to confrontation you can be one to retreat into your shell (or airing cupboard), but if you choose your friends wisely you're a dependable asset to them.

- ★ **Best traits:** Loyalty; patience; emotional intelligence.

- ★ **Worst traits:** Narcissism; possessiveness; pessimism.

- ★ **Likes:** Rubbing their face on their human; giving love-headbutts.

- ★ **Dislikes:** Sharing their human.

- ★ **Strengths:** Dependability; strength in conviction.

- ★ **Weaknesses:** Emotional rather than logical; retreats from "trouble".

# RELATIONSHIPS

## *Friends and enemies*

Who's that chasing a ball when you fancy a bit of peace?
Who's that raking their claws down the sofa when you're
lying down with your eyes closed? You like a certain
steadiness, a constancy to things, and this puts you at odds
with the caffeinated-on-life Aquarius. They're the sort of
friend you'll squeeze yourself down a narrow hole to avoid.

What you need is a Taurus. They're a big, sturdy bull;
you're a firm, hardy crab. Your shared need for stability
and security make you excellent friends. Whether you're
sleeping on a bed, sleeping in a box or sleeping on a shower
curtain that's somehow ended up clawed down and on the
floor, your best Taurus-bud will give you the safest catnap
you could want.

## Love and sex

A Cancer cat's favourite time is when things are harmonious and "just so". Beware, then, an impulsive and dominating sign such as Aries. When things get tense (like when you need to pass each other and both refuse to use the ample space either side) your Aries will get testy, and, as the crab retreats into its shell, so you'll (adorably) cover your face with your paws and wait for it to be over.

Why not shoot for a more solid, understanding time with a Virgo? You're both sensitive, both prioritize taking care of family and loved ones and both communicate adroitly when you feel safe, meaning your paws can be used less for hiding and more for squishing flies.

# With humans

Cancer signs like consistency so, naturally, the duality-led indecision of Gemini makes for a bad pairing. Does this basket look better for you? This size cat flap? This collar? This food? There are only so many laundry hampers you can escape to before you're discovered and the inquisition resumes. Gemini is not the one.

Scorpio humans like to feel desirable and wanted, and this turns your often-maligned possessiveness into your greatest strength. Some humans may not appreciate how uncomfortable you're able to make any guests they wish to have over for the evening, but Scorpios see this as the highest compliment. They are yours, which pleases them and makes them more loyal, which in turn pleases you. Give that human the slow-blink they deserve.

# RISING STARS AND PLANETS

Did last year leave you feeling like the tide was washing over you in one moment, and washing you out the next? Well, this is your time to take the power back! The sun spends some time in your sign in early summer and settles things down nicely – the perfect time to come out of your shell and grab life! Find a shed, climb on top it and meow for the world to hear!

## HOROSCOPE

After a stressful year, it's time to look after your health. Try new ways of stretching, new ways of sleeping, even new ways of eating (like actually clearing your bowl, instead of eating maybe a quarter, looking at your human like something has happened and it's their fault, and then slinking away). Technology also plays a key role in your year so be sure to fill keyboards with your hair, lick some smartphones, ride around on those automatic vacuum cleaners and see what it brings!

# LEO

## 23 JULY – 22 AUGUST

**Symbol:** The Lion
**Element:** Fire
**Ruling planet:** The Sun

**Gem stone:** Golden topaz
**Colour:** Gold
**Lucky number:** 17

# **PERSONALITY**

## Overview

Sound the trumpets and ring the bells: here comes Leo! Your passion and warmth draws others to you like catnip – you're never short of friends and never shy to take the lead. Sometimes being noticed is more of a need than a joy for you, but don't worry if you've not had your hero's welcome this morning: objects at the edges of tables are just heralding crashes waiting to happen.

★ **Best traits:** Passionate; warm-hearted; magnetic.

★ **Worst traits:** Arrogant; aggressive; domineering.

★ **Likes:** Taking the lead; being fussed over; being optimistic.

★ **Dislikes:** Following others; compromising.

★ **Strengths:** Charisma; creativity; confidence.

★ **Weaknesses:** Proud; stubborn; lazy.

# RELATIONSHIPS

## Friends and enemies

As a Leo, you live a life balanced between extremes. Your charisma can become attention-seeking; your confidence and leadership, such attractive qualities, can put others in the shade. Your worst traits can sting a jealous Scorpio, who would share with a lesser personality but may feel threatened by your glory. And your constant basking in that glory.

Best to seek a like mind. A mind that is cool, relaxed and doesn't require the constant attention of the human in the house. Well, until that attention decides to focus on something else. And then it *super* needs it! What you need is a partner in crime: a cat who loves life, loves living big and makes themselves unmissable, just when your human thinks it's safe to look away. Enter Gemini, and see a lasting friendship begin.

# *Love and sex*

Taurus is sturdy, conservative and careful. They spend most of their time living in the future, trying to foresee problems to give themselves the best chance to react. In this relationship, nine times out of ten, that problem will be you. You live in the present, led by heart and courage, and any studious reflection is trampled under-paw as you bound head first into the next misadventure.

No, no. What you need is a cat who sees the world as you do. A cat who sees leftover human food not as a treat but as their birthright; who sees not a pile of clean laundry but a throne to sit upon. You need decadence, dominance, dynamism – even more, you need a cat who needs as passionately as you do. That's right – your perfect match is a strutting, swaggering Aries.

# With humans

Your creativity is one of your most appealing strengths; a strength that a more practical-minded Capricorn person likely won't understand. You look at a foot and your creative mind sees an invader, or an evil puppet, or a flat, dry fish, and you react bravely either by batting or biting it down. Capricorns don't see the world like you do. They just see a foot, and your attacks will not be well-received.

A Sagittarius, on the other hand. Well, now you're talking. Sagittarians have an intense love of adventure. When you rock up at home in the dead of night, covered in leaves and bits of twig, this human will just give you a knowing nod and welcome you back. Plus, they respect your curiosity. They *know* you don't want to eat their salad or their chocolate cake, but you're royalty to them, and they'll always let you try it just in case.

# RISING STARS AND PLANETS

Your year begins with a supermoon, which will spotlight your true feelings. As a Leo, you may be thinking, "Great – I love a spotlight!" That's true, but it'll shine on your faux pas as well as your successes, so prepare to brag about your achievements ("caught one *this* big; no, *twice* that size!") but also to repackage that slip off the wall or that stumble into your dinner as totally cool and on purpose.

# HOROSCOPE

Last year was a good year, and you're riding the crest of a wave. Of course you are! But do you know what's difficult about being well-groomed, great-looking and generally awesome? Stagnation. It might feel like there's little room to grow but keep an eye out for challenges that will help you develop. Instead of watching with complete apathy as that string dangles, try to grab it; instead of urinating on the newspaper, try doing the crossword. Keep sharp, and stay at your brilliant best!

# VIRGO

## 23 AUGUST – 22 SEPTEMBER

**Symbol:** The Maiden

**Element:** Earth

**Ruling planet:** Mercury

**Gem stone:** Garnet

**Colours:** Green and brown

**Lucky number:** 7

# PERSONALITY

## *Overview*

You have a lot of love to give. Whether it's rubbing your face on people, kneading with your paws or licking with your scratchy tongue, you're not afraid to show affection to those closest to you. Sometimes your honesty tips into unwelcome criticism. But sometimes it doesn't! And your glass is half full, so let's think of it like that.

★ **Best traits:** Practical; dutiful; trustworthy.

★ **Worst traits:** Critical of self and others; freely expresses criticism.

★ **Likes:** Helping others; winning people over by speech/meows.

★ **Dislikes:** Recognition for good deeds; all the worries they have.

★ **Strengths:** Meticulous; dependable; logical.

★ **Weaknesses:** Perfectionism; obsessiveness; temperamental.

# RELATIONSHIPS

## *Friends and enemies*

Your analytical, critical nature means you examine things closely. Your human has just put something in front of you: it may be a small ball or felt mouse. Aren't felt mice interesting, you think. You know they're not real but are still compelled to attack in the traditional fashion. What does this say about the nature... oh, an Aries is flinging the toy around, and now it's disappeared under the sofa with dozens of other toys this has happened to. They are not concerned with deep thinking. Steer clear.

It isn't only things your human has provided that captivate. Whether it's a shoe beneath the stairs, a bucket in the garden or a video-game controller, everything is interesting to you. But also, you have that quirk of calmly investigating something for up to half a minute before making the flash decision that *this is danger* and bolting a few feet away from it. When frights can come from anywhere, a sturdy Cancer bestie can be there to protect and reassure you as you continue your important studies.

## Love and sex

Some cats will adore your attention to detail and thoughtful feedback to help them improve. Nobody's perfect, right? Well, no – but some signs would like to *think* they are. Picture the scene: you and a Leo, lying side by side, bellies pointed skyward. They've just demonstrated all their best moves and are looking like the cat who got the cream. Then you roll over and systematically pick apart their performance, with helpful hints for next time. Game. Over.

You need a cat with broad shoulders. The best partner for you isn't one who sees themselves as perfect but who aims for a perfect *balance* in all areas of their life. When this is the goal, that attention to detail, that thoughtful feedback will actually help them keep things solid, consistent and effectively ticking over. Taurus might not be the most sexually adventurous sign, but you just get each other. Happy homebuilding.

## With humans

Gemini humans can be prone to wild flights of fancy, which can often be expressed by spending lots of money on ostentatious furniture. Your Virgo analysis and attention to detail will help you to identify which of these pieces of furniture is the most valuable and will therefore make the perfect scratching spot for you. You can see how this has the potential to not work out.

In life, we need different things from different species under different signs. So it may surprise you to learn that your sexual opposite, the prideful Leo, is actually your perfect human counterpart. Leos love attention and can be very vain. Your prolonged, studious staring may weird out some humans, but Leo will take it as the highest form of flattery and reward you with treats and affection.

# RISING STARS AND PLANETS

Your natural clear-headedness is clouded by emotion and sentimentality with the appearance of January's full moon. Normally, a new scratch-post is a great thing. Mmm, scratchy! But remember the old one? Remember all those incredible stretches you had against it? You're missing it now, right? Fear not: these lines of thinking will align as the year progresses, and you can remember the good times while getting stuck into something new (and scratchy!).

# HOROSCOPE

Self-care is the order of the day for you as far as this year goes. You've studied, you've examined, you've learned more than most kitties do in a lifetime. But now it's time to do you. Get plenty of belly rubs, be extra persistent when your human is eating something they don't want to share and give yourself plenty of long, luxurious washes (being mindful to hack the spittle-hairballs back out onto the carpet).

# LIBRA

23 SEPTEMBER – 22 OCTOBER

**Symbol:** The Scales
**Element:** Air
**Ruling planet:** Venus

**Gem stone:** Bloodstone
**Colours:** Pink and light blue
**Lucky number:** 5

# PERSONALITY

## *Overview*

Librans are all about peace, justice and balance. If a human hears two cats mewling like mad before suddenly falling silent, chances are a Libran happened by and defused the situation. Your ability to see things from both sides can make you indecisive, but you can always go and nap in the sun while you wait for an answer to come.

- ★ **Best traits:** Balanced; charming; fun-seeking; affectionate.

- ★ **Worst traits:** Aloof; hasty; indecisive.

- ★ **Likes:** Equilibrium; head scratches.

- ★ **Dislikes:** Making important choices; being alone.

- ★ **Strengths:** Diplomatic; graceful; peace-loving.

- ★ **Weaknesses:** Unreliable; stubborn; idealistic.

# RELATIONSHIPS

## *Friends and enemies*

Cancer, the crab, carries their home with them at all times. Their shell represents stability, familiarity and safety. They know what they like, they feel comfortable when they stick to that and they exercise caution when encountering unfamiliar people. The shell also acts as a barrier, and they can be cagey and hard to bond with. That just isn't you.

You're an outgoing kind of moggy. First thing in the morning, after breakfast and a good stretch, you're through the cat flap and out meeting new friends. And there are so many hotspots, so many friends: the skittish cat you always catch though the window, the squinty cat swishing his tail from the garden wall and, of course, the nightly get-together by the supermarket bins. There are many extroverted allies in the Zodiac but Aquarius is the least attention-seeking and the most into it for the same reasons as you: being a social cat.

# Love and sex

You're out having fun through the day and long into the night. One second the sun is high in the sky, the next it's gone and you're stalking home by streetlight. Some people would call this "fun" or "impulsive". Others would call it "unreliable". As a solid, dependable bull, a Taurus partner is likely to be waiting, paws on hips, for answers as to where you've been. The sex after that is only going to go one way. If it happens at all.

You don't mind the odd night in – you just don't want to be tied down or penned in, so who better to help you on this quest than The Twins of Gemini? Geminis themselves have an outgoing, sociable personality, but their excellent communication skills could also help you achieve a finer balance and see the upsides of a night spent in. And with the fizzing chemistry between you, you shouldn't need much convincing, tiger.

## With humans

Pisces humans are generally homebodies and, being naturally creative, may forego a cat flap in favour of assuming you'll devise some brilliant method of entry yourself. But you won't – you'll just sit by the window, or the door, and mewl until your tired human gets out of bed and lets you in. They'll want company in the lounge and you'll want freedom by the bins: this one is not made to last.

You're affectionate and charming, and Sagittarius humans love this about you. They become enchanted with your grace, your poise and your friendliness, and this plays to your advantage as your smitten owner overlooks your hasty and indecisive nature. When you eagerly devour their latest offering of wet food only to decide days later, when they come home with a whole case, that not only is it not your favourite but you simply won't eat it at all, they'll be so utterly charmed with your quirks that they'll just laugh and get you something else. Lovely.

# RISING STARS AND PLANETS

When soothing Venus enters your sign in the middle of September, you'll feel your most harmonious *and* your most balanced. These are your strengths, so prepare to feel wonderfully at peace. There's a full moon during the spring equinox, which is a time for repairing broken bonds. So if you're emotionally sore from your human trying to bathe you (and they're physically sore as a result), maybe give them a little headbutt to say all is forgiven.

## HOROSCOPE

With your silver tongue and persuasive style of chat, other cats can't help but be drawn to you. However, you're not always letting them see the real you. Sure, you can tell them that you're wearing that flowery collar ironically; sure, you can say that you own the house and the human stays with *you*. Or you can take a chance, be authentic and let this be the year that others see your true self!

# SCORPIO

### 23 OCTOBER – 21 NOVEMBER

**Symbol:** The Scorpion
**Element:** Water
**Ruling planet:** Pluto

**Gem stone:** Onyx
**Colour:** Black
**Lucky number:** 13

# **PERSONALITY**

## *Overview*

You're a self-confident, passionate sign that loves with intensity. Okay, it can border on a possessiveness that makes you the cat every owner's partner has been warned about. But you can also be very friendly. So play nice.

★ **Best traits:** Assertive; trustworthy; imaginative; friendly.

★ **Worst traits:** Secretive; temperamental; vengeful.

★ **Likes:** Having their ego stroked; leading; sensuousness.

★ **Dislikes:** Being instructed; sharing their human.

★ **Strengths:** Passionate; caring; energetic.

★ **Weaknesses:** Scheming; jealousy; temperamental.

# RELATIONSHIPS

## *Friends and enemies*

You know how to make others feel special. You desire meaningful connections and your intense, starey eye contact makes others feel like they're the only other cat in the room. Soothe them, charm them and soon they're eating out of your paw and you've learned an awful lot about what the humans next door get up to when the drapes are shut. Ignore, then, the outgoing yet flitty Aquarius. They'll be leaning on a wall, scanning the street for the next interesting story. You want quality, they want quantity. Hiss.

Scorpios are an imaginative bunch. Others may diligently slurp their dinner and be (mostly) content, while Scorpios are thinking of the ham on the counter, or the chicken carcass in the bin, and wondering "What if...?" So who best to help? Another dreamer won't help get things done. And a bundle of energy is no use without direction. You need practicality, planning – somebody who can see: that broom can be climbed, that bin is a little off-centre. And a bit of muscle wouldn't hurt either. Get a Taurus on side and share in your spoils together.

## *Love and sex*

The love and sex of Scorpio is a story of playing against type. Due to your assertiveness and inclination to lead, you'd imagine a bold Leo lover would be just what you want. However, you've got a side of you that doesn't like to be in the shade, and a Leo loves nothing more than having all eyes on them. Nobody puts kitty in a corner.

Generally, Cancer shies away from the more gregarious signs, intimidated by their brashness and confidence. You're an outgoing personality, no mistaking it, but with the caveat that you wear your jealousy and possessiveness on your sleeve, which makes you appear more vulnerable and knowable to the Crab. In return, their honesty and dedication will calm that side of you, creating something potentially special.

# With humans

Geminis are a sociable sort and will likely have friends over all the time. This won't sit well with your jealous, possessive side. While, to you, knocking over plants, ornaments and coffee mugs and generally using the sideboards as a kind of shooting gallery is just your way of saying "show me some attention, please", this is one trait a Gemini just isn't going to change.

Pisces are the poets, the romantics, the deep lovers of the Zodiac, and while it isn't *likely* you'll hop through the cat flap to find a cat-sized dinner table set up with tiny candles, a small glass of organic milk and a little silver platter with your favourite food on it, they'll love you enough that you can never rule it out.

# RISING STARS AND PLANETS

Good news, Scorpio: Mars not only stays direct for the entire next year, but also crosses into Aries, giving you the strength and drive to achieve your goals! So, get out there and catch that pesky dot, upgrade your basket to that big, comfy bed and climb that tree across the street (remember, it's the getting up that takes the effort – it's your human's concern how you get down).

# HOROSCOPE

Uranus, that wildcard, is showing up in your chart this year, meaning all sexual bets are off. You've always had a particular type – the type of cat who, when its human puts one of those shirt-collar/bow-tie combos around its neck, doesn't immediately flail it back off. Someone steady, who loves you unconditionally and doesn't raise your green-eyed monster. This year, look outside the box – try Leo, try Aries, try being a fierce and strong-willed feline! If there was ever a chance to sample the full flavours the Zodiac has to offer, it's now!

# SAGITTARIUS

## 22 NOVEMBER – 21 DECEMBER

**Symbol:** The Archer
**Element:** Fire
**Ruling planet:** Jupiter

**Gem stone:** Amethyst
**Colour:** Purple
**Lucky number:** 26

# **PERSONALITY**

## *Overview*

As the sign of the Archer, you're a driven individual who is focused on achieving your targets. The main one is travel: you're a passionate voyager and will enthusiastically go anywhere, anyhow. Unless it's to the vets in one of those carry-cages. But other than that you're pretty fearless.

★ **Best traits:** Cheerful; energetic; ambitious.

★ **Worst traits:** Inflexible; impatient; unemotional.

★ **Likes:** Journeys; adventures; rearing up and putting their paws on TV shows about travel.

★ **Dislikes:** Too many choices; life in the slow lane.

★ **Strengths:** Wanderlust; independence; friendliness.

★ **Weaknesses:** Temperamental; restless; averse to criticism.

# RELATIONSHIPS

## Friends and enemies

You love action and adventure, something new every day. But, you know, who doesn't? Taurus. You're jazzed to get outside and explore the world with your buddy. You sit by the door, Taurus sits by the door, the human opens the door... and Taurus continues to sit. Thinking, deciding. Confusing the human. All the while you hop from paw to paw, eager to just get *going*. Leave Taurus to think with a cat who is a little less *now*.

Because you're a fizzing firecracker of a feline, who better to supercharge that energy than a wild-at-heart Aries? Not only do they match your vigour, they're as fun-loving as you are and equally as optimistic. Some cats may doubt that you can shred every totally fun roll of toilet paper in the bathroom before someone gets home. Your Aries pal not only knows you'll get the job done, but you'll do it in time to look utterly indifferent for your human when they get home.

## Love and sex

You've got energy, you've got ambition; you've got a hundred thoughts as a result. Can you eat what you found on the floor? Can you play with that ball; catch that dot; maul those shoelaces? You've got a lot to get done, which would leave a poor pragmatic Capricorn shouldering the daily grind of cat life, like leaving hair everywhere or eating half the food you're given and leaving the rest. They'll resent you; you'll be jumping off stuff and won't notice. Move along, nothing to see here.

Cheerfulness and friendliness aren't often number one on the list of "sexy traits in a partner". Unless, of course, you're a Pisces. These warm yet sensitive souls will love that they're not absorbing the vibe off some sourpuss, and the rigidity that would turn off more spontaneous signs will be deeply reassuring to them. In return, you get openness to match candour, creativity for your travels and schemes, and a very attentive lover. Not a bad deal at all.

## With humans

Leo humans like to look good. They like long, luxurious showers, blow-drying their hair, straightening or curling their hair, admiring their hair. And that's before they've even decided what to wear (and admired their stellar choice in clothes after). All the while you're waiting for breakfast, for the door to be opened, for your tray to be cleaned. You're too impatient for that, and your Leo person will not appreciate you revengefully swiping their hairspray to the floor.

Aquarius humans share your independence, your good-naturedness and your love of travel. They get it when you want to sit a few feet away instead of right on their lap, or you want to chill in a box or under a trampoline in the garden. And when the time comes for them to head off and see the world, they're the one sign that will always have your cat-passport in their rucksack right next to theirs.

# RISING STARS AND PLANETS

Things can be chaotic in the life of a cat: vacuum cleaners whirring, human feet stumbling, naps being disturbed. Praise be to the full moon in June and the arrival of Jupiter, which will calm your nerves and help you see that those things happen for a reason: humans stumble through lack of feline grace, vacuum cleaners whirr to suck your loose hair from the carpet and naps are disturbed because... no, okay. There's no reason for that.

# HOROSCOPE

Not all years are cream and biscuits and naps, and last year may have been tough. But New Year, new you! So be tough, be strict and grab happiness. Encourage your human to pick you out a new collar. Embrace a new diet and only eat from the garbage at weekends. The sun will enter your sign late this year, giving you renewed energy: instead of just running madly through the house at 1 a.m., you could go for a second sprint at 4 a.m.! The possibilities are endless. How exciting!

# CAPRICORN

## 22 DECEMBER – 19 JANUARY

**Symbol:** The Goat
**Element:** Earth
**Ruling planet:** Saturn

**Gem stone:** Tiger's eye
**Colours:** Grey and brown
**Lucky number:** 25

# PERSONALITY

## Overview

You're reliable and a good laugh, and you know your own mind. "Diva?" Hah! That's just something people say when they don't understand you. Alright, so you like to make sure things are done a certain way, and that certain way *is* often your way. But we've all got a little "Pawdrey Hepburn" in us, right?

★ **Best traits:** Dependable; ambitious; disciplined; humorous.

★ **Worst traits:** Headstrong; stubborn; autocratic.

★ **Likes:** Persevering; pursuing success.

★ **Dislikes:** Leaving their comfort zone; having their head scratched when they're trying to be serious.

★ **Strengths:** Practicality; trustworthiness; reliability.

★ **Weaknesses:** Suspicious; reserved; slow to ask for help.

# RELATIONSHIPS

## Friends and enemies

It's nice when friends are reliable, stable and practical. So Aries should probably go find a different playmate. Yes, you're supposed to have nine lives; yes, you're supposed to always land on your feet. But you're a "*What if?*" kind of a cat, and Aries is more of a "*What now?*" Leave them to work that out for themselves.

Virgos, like you, are practical, reliable and clear-headed. All very good. But also, like you, Virgos know how to keep a secret and like to keep a low profile. So, when your human finds cat litter scuffed and kicked an impressive distance from the litter tray, said low profile will likely convince them it could have been anyone, while you both stare with knowing eyes from behind a plant in the corner.

# Love and sex

Some Zodiac signs are stubborn. There's no escaping that. But there are different flavours: stubborn and angry, stubborn and prideful, stubborn and hissy. Cancer is non-confrontational, and so are you, meaning your stubbornness results in prolonged, ineffective staring. And as far as stoking things for a night of passion goes, unbroken, mildly annoyed staring isn't going to get anyone purring.

The aspect of you that could be described as "dictatorial" might imagine an ideal partner as a sign that's a bit of a pushover. Someone who puts you first, bends to your will. However, there's more to you than that, and your headstrong, humorous, practical side will want a lover, not a flunky. Scuttle forward assertive, temperamental Scorpio. They'll keep you on your toes, keep your ego in check and make sparks fly between the sheets.

## With humans

Christmas comes – your Taurus human receives lots of dull gifts in lots of lovely big boxes. Every cat loves a box, but you're ambitious. That's your thing. You could be mayor of a whole cardboard town! Nap in the library, nap in the town hall. Endless possibilities. But, oh no – straight-old Taurus doesn't see this and bins the lot. Bah.

Some humans appreciate your better, trustworthy qualities: from trusting you to do "your business" where you should, to trusting that when you beg and plead for love and attention you actually want it and won't immediately scratch them when they come near. Equally, you want to trust that when your human comes for cuddles you won't suddenly find yourself fighting out of a scarily tight novelty jumper. Get a Pisces and revel in honesty, trust and someone creative enough to see your box-town idea.

# RISING STARS AND PLANETS

Pluto moves directly into your sign in October – the perfect opportunity to reassess relationships, rebuild or start over. Did you ever get to know that bulky cat who sits, panting, on the porch a few houses down and who you skitter nervously past? Or the ginger cat you hiss at in the garden "just cos?" Saturn will enter your sign to beef up your chances of success. This is the year to embrace change!

# HOROSCOPE

Last year it felt refreshing to put others first, but it's taken a toll and you can't force compatibility. That cautious Taurus who wants to keep your mouse toy in good condition rather than mindlessly wreck it? That outgoing Gemini who won't let you get a meow in edgeways? You've put in the hours, done your time, and if it isn't working for you, then don't be afraid to fling that mouse, meow in their face and meet others that appreciate you for who you are!

# AQUARIUS

## 20 JANUARY – 18 FEBRUARY

**Symbol:** The Water-Bearer
**Element:** Air
**Ruling planet:** Uranus

**Gem stone:** Blue obsidian
**Colour:** Blue
**Lucky number:** 8

# **PERSONALITY**

## *Overview*

Those who fall under the Capricorn sign are curious, creative and independent. There might be food in that bin bag; but what else might be in there? Mice? Birds? The meaning of life? You want to know about the world, and your defiant streak means you'll often just poke your head in somewhere and find out what's going on.

★ **Best traits:** Independent; inventive; spontaneous; inquisitive.

★ **Worst traits:** Obstinate; aloof; unemotional.

★ **Likes:** Exploring the back of the sofa.

★ **Dislikes:** Being called in before they're ready.

★ **Strengths:** Creative; honest; intellectual.

★ **Weaknesses:** Rebellious; uncompromising; temperamental.

# **RELATIONSHIPS**

## *Friends and enemies*

Isn't it fascinating when humans use their toilet? Standing there, sitting there – you could just sit, stare and make them feel self-conscious for hours. But your inquisitive nature doesn't end there. They've flushed, they've gone and they've left the seat up! The mystery! It's worth hopping up there to take a look, and it's at times like these, with your head halfway in the bowl, that you just don't want your best friend behind you to be a mischievous Aries.

Virgos are much more trustworthy and have an innate curiosity like yours. Far from nudging you over the side, they'd be springing up to that porcelain rim and wondering, too, what it all means. And when you're done with that there are just as many questions to ask when humans are in the bath, or are eating food you've never tried, or when they've left their shoes unattended. You've got a lot to explore together.

## Love and sex

You'd imagine that your inherent creativity would make you and Pisces a playful match made in heaven. For both of you, any bouncing ball, flailing sock or trailing towel is endlessly fun to enjoy. But Pisces needs clear and obvious love, and your unemotional and indifferent side (and your need to sit comfortably out of reach of anything that tries too hard to show you affection) is bound to hurt some feelings.

With a Gemini, you can have your delicious sachet of meat-and-jelly *and* eat it. While not so creative themselves, Geminis are fascinated by ideas. What *is* inside a slipper? And how badly do you have to savage it to find out? But they're also fiercely independent and this helps you find a shared harmony in your own space, in separate laundry baskets at opposite ends of the house.

## With humans

Sagittarian humans love adventure. They're always off on one journey or another, but, owing to their inflexible and rigid nature, the time of departure is often set in stone. And you're a rebellious, obstinate sort. I mean, you can *hear* your name being called, but you're having a nice time flopped out in the cold, pitch-black garden a few houses away. Someone has to budge. And whoever does won't take it well.

You're independent, aloof and uncompromising. You like a bit of affection, but you like it on your terms, and your terms are almost exclusively "thirty seconds before your human wants to move". Do you know who'll get that? Bold, independent, uncompromising Leo. Because that's probably what they're like with *their* partner.

# RISING STARS AND PLANETS

This year your planet, Uranus, completes its slow transition from wild Aries into contented Taurus. If you've made any decisions in the heat of the moment, now is the time to stop and ask yourself some questions. Do I really hate that brand of food? Is it really either me or the plant in the hall? Why am I massacring every pair of shoes in the house? Take your time and don't beat yourself up. It's possible those shoes deserved it.

## HOROSCOPE

Did you have a bit of a "no" year last year? Perhaps there were opportunities, potential friendships and unusual cuisines that you sniffed for a micro-second before deciding "nope" and sloping away. Comfort zones are nice, but so might be that hole you could squeeze through in the back fence, or that pleasant-looking cat you see at the vet's, or that posh cat food that you see even your human looking at and thinking "Hmm...?" Get out there, sniff life with a little excitement and make this your "yes" year!

# PISCES

## 19 FEBRUARY – 20 MARCH

**Symbol:** The (delicious) Fish
**Element:** Water
**Ruling planet:** Neptune

**Gem stone:** Turquoise
**Colour:** Light green
**Lucky number:** 14

# **PERSONALITY**

## Overview

You're the accepting, easy-going final sign of the Zodiac. You have empathy, gentleness and a lot of care in you. This can make you prone to having your feelings hurt, but as long as others are respectful and gentle, you are fiercely loyal and have the creativity to weave endless tales of brave moggies and big fish.

★ **Best traits:** Empathetic; compassionate; wise; a dreamer.

★ **Worst traits:** Unrealistic; overly trusting.

★ **Likes:** Chasing butterflies.

★ **Dislikes:** Rarely catching them.

★ **Strengths:** Ability to knead any human into submission.

★ **Weaknesses:** Chasing string wherever it leads.

# RELATIONSHIPS

## *Friends and enemies*

The last sign on your list for lasting friendship is an extroverted, excitable Libran. When you want to dream your dreams and relax for the "napping" part of the day (for example the middle 90 per cent) your Libra will be craving attention, huffing and snorting and skipping about and batting your tail and face. How is anyone supposed to sleep with that going on?

Dreaming is a lovely, harmless trait, right? Well, not always. Dreams can't be achieved without a little curiosity, and we all know what *that* does to you if you have four legs and your breath smells like fish. Find yourself a diligent, pragmatic Capricorn, and ask for their wise words when your next dream involves sticking your head in the goldfish bowl.

## *Love and sex*

Gemini? Gemi-no. Their frivolous, changeable nature can detract from the committed pursuits of a Pisces. Pisceans might love to chase a butterfly, but they're at least dedicated to the task at hand. Geminis will chase for a bit and the next minute be washing themselves like idiots or rolling about in the sun.

Scorpios. Passionate. Powerful. A furry, fiery, flashbang ball of... water? That's right – you and that late October love-cat from the lawn next door are elementally compatible. You both like to explore boundaries: be that mindful, playful or sexual. And you guys are cats – that's a lot of sexual boundaries.

## With humans

Your warm Piscean empathy will help you build strong bonds with a Cancer-signed human who matches your compassion and loves to be loved. A hop on the bed and some firm, enthusiastic paw-smushes will give your food-giver the reassurance to love you with all their heart and, crucially, to keep giving you food.

Best, however, to skip the Sagittarius breed of people. They love freedom and adventure and being a rolling stone, and the kneading required to secure tasty morsels is much harder when your human is always somewhere else.

# RISING STARS AND PLANETS

Pisces is generally a gentle soul but you'll be especially caring and kind as your ruler, Neptune, sits in your sign the whole year through. Be nice, but also, importantly, don't be naive with it: if a wandering cat from another block approaches and eats your dinner with the promise that you can have his the day after, let's face it – you probably won't see that cat again. Stay clear-headed and you can develop some great, long-lasting relationships!

## HOROSCOPE

Three planets are due to pass through the friendship region of your chart this year, sending your social circle into the stratosphere and potentially pairing you up with some pretty big names! Be those local movie stars Catalie Portman and Cindy Clawford, singer Meowly Cyrus or even dashing rebel Litter-Tray Guevara, you've got an exciting year ahead! Get out there and make your star shine!

# TAROT READINGS

### Aries – The Emperor

Like the royal figure on your card, use your influence
and charm to make people fall at your feet!

.....................................................................

### Taurus – The Hierophant

This card represents knowledge from a
teacher. There's more than one way to skin
a cat, and they'll show you all of them!

.....................................................................

### Gemini – The Lovers

This indicates a moral choice. You might urinate in your
human's rucksack, but should you stay and fess up?

.....................................................................

### Cancer – The Chariot

This will chart a path above the conflicts you
face in life. Bonus: you can grandly meow
the theme to *Chariots of Fire* as you go.

### Leo – Strength

Because what else would it be? Physical,
emotional, spiritual – whatever you need this
year, "Strength" has got you covered!

..................................................................

### Virgo – The Hermit

Retreat within yourself and make exciting
new discoveries. Perhaps you'll realize
you like dogs. Or thrash metal!

..................................................................

### Libra – Justice

Put your feelings and emotions aside and
do the right thing. Unless you're really,
really tired. Then just have a nap.

..................................................................

### Scorpio – Death

Don't worry – this actually just means "transformation".
Like how you can transform that mouse in the
kitchen into a present for your human!

### Sagittarius – Temperance

You are a gifted mediator, arriving to end disputes.
Who gets the spot in front of the fire? You do!

........................................................................

### Capricorn – The Devil

Reflect on any negativity: see it, understand it and
then do some cat-judo to wrestle it into submission.

........................................................................

### Aquarius – The Star

This focuses you on optimism and wishes. It's also small
and twinkly and just out of reach. Like the ultimate fly.

........................................................................

### Pisces – The Moon

This represents a creature of ever-changing moods,
and you'll embody this as you go from apathetic,
to indifferent, to blasé, to uninterested.

*Cats are connoisseurs of comfort.*

JAMES HERRIOT

# PAW READINGS

### Aries

Your jelly-bean toes show... you freely
express your feelings. See also: the red marks
on your human's hands and arms.

........................................

### Taurus

Your jelly-bean toes show... your zen outlook
and good handle on your emotions. You should
turn those claws to clipping bonsai trees.

........................................

### Gemini

Your jelly-bean toes show... many relationships or
lovers. And good for you. They still haven't invented
cat-weddings yet, so just go do your thing.

........................................

### Cancer

Your jelly-bean toes show... short attention span.
But look on the bright– oh, you've wandered off.

### Leo

Your jelly-bean toes show... a sleek, handsome
figure on your heart line. Don't get too
excited – chances are it's just you.

......................................................

### Virgo

Your jelly-bean toes show... your thinking is clear and
focused. Picture the nap, want the nap, *be* the nap.

......................................................

### Libra

Your jelly-bean toes show... you think realistically.
You just watch that fly hitting the window
over and over. It'll tire itself out soon...

......................................................

### Scorpio

Your jelly-bean toes show... momentous decisions.
Sleep before food? Or food before sleep?

### Sagittarius

Your jelly-bean toes show... you have great changes coming. What's new, pussycat?

................................................................

### Capricorn

Your jelly-bean toes show... you are often tired. Which, bearing in mind you're a cat, gives you every right to feel you're being singled out.

................................................................

### Aquarius

Your jelly-bean toes show... you're easily flattered. And who wouldn't be with such adorable little toesies!

................................................................

### Pisces

Your jelly-bean toes show... you're a self-made individual. And why not – that idea of yours where cats race on automated vacuum cleaners is pretty good.

## CONCLUSION

Well – what a vast, cosmic journey. Whoever you are, whatever your sign, you have a big and exciting year ahead! Or do you? Of course, if you're planning to lie very still with your eyes closed for the best part of twelve months, well, you can't expect too many of those lofty ambitions to be reached. Just remember – this book can only show you the cat flap. It is still up to you to saunter through it. Good luck, and make it a meow-vellous year!

If you're interested in finding out more about our books, find us on Facebook at **Summersdale Publishers** and follow us on Twitter at **@Summersdale**.

# www.summersdale.com